Why He Won't Marry You

Alexander J. Patrick

ISBN: 1523908505
ISBN-13: 978-1523908509

DEDICATION

I would like to dedicate this book to my son Alex. You are too young to understand all this book entails. However, I am writing it with your future wife in mind. May you always treat women with respect and honor. May you not fall into the traps that this world has set up for you. Your father made a lot of mistakes that you don't have to. One day when you are old enough, I hope you will read this book and it will help you skip the mistakes I made. It will help you to desire to be a husband and a God fearing man.

CONTENTS

ACKNOWLEDGMENTS

I would like to first and foremost thank God for giving me the gift of wisdom and creativity. I could not write this book without His guidance and divine assistance. I would like to acknowledge my church family, who is always supportive in my ventures to impact the community for the better. There are few people who gave me an extra push to write this book. I don't want to call any names because I may leave someone out. However, you know who you are and if in any way you indirectly suggested or directly challenged me to begin writing. I want to thank you from the bottom of my heart. Your belief in me sparked a burden to come out of my shell and share what's in my heart. Thank you for challenging me to expand my gifts into authorship. To my mother Sarah Patrick, thank you for all of your prayers over the years. For all the times that I gave you every reason to give up on me, I know you never stopped praying. My life today as a pastor and now as an author is an answer to your prayers. I am so humbled and grateful that the Lord saw fit to make you my mother. Last but certainly not least, my wife Ashley Patrick. You have helped me in more ways than you will ever realize. Through being your husband, I have found my way to complete manhood and divine purpose. The way you love me brings out the best in me, and I pray you will be proud of me as I embark upon this journey of writing the first of many books.

INTRODUCTION

Women all over the country are asking two questions:

1.   Where are all the single men?

2.   Why don't they want to get married?

My name is Alexander J. Patrick and I pastor a local church and provide pre-marital and marital counseling as part of my pastoral responsibility. This book is designed to answer these two questions. Many of the young women in my church and in the community seem to all have similar concerns. "When will I find my equal"? The notion is I worked hard on getting myself together. I am emotionally and spiritually stable, but still feel incomplete. I have built a wonderful career, I have a great church family, plenty of family and friends, but I am ready to start a family. If this sounds familiar to you and you can relate, then I wrote this book just for you. I want to take some time to explain from the male perspective why men are hesitant to get married. As a pastor and married man, of course I am an advocate for marriage. However, I cannot ignore the immense amount of disconnects there are from the female perspective of marriage and the male perspective of marriage. <u>In most cases when a female in her 30's thinks about marriage she is envisioning an imaginary biological clock ticking and running out of time. When a man in his 30's is thinking about marriage, he sees the same clock but it is not running out of time......it's more like a bomb timer ticking down the seconds until his life is blown up!</u> In other words women typically see marriage as the beginning, and men see it as the end. See the difference? In this book I will attempt to explain the context in the difference of perspectives and hopefully young adults who are single or dating can find balance in their pursuit of healthy relationships and eventually healthy marriages.

I would like to be clear. This book is not about what's wrong with women! This book is about why men struggle with monogamy and marriage. Often times, women spend a great deal of their adult life in bondage to the thoughts that their singleness is related to inadequacy. Many women suffer with the insecurity that because they are not married yet, they are in some way not good enough. Not to mention all the women who have been a part of infidelity who feel that it was somehow all their fault. That could not be any further from the truth. The truth is, in most cases a man's lack of desire to get married or his inability to remain monogamous has nothing to do with you. A lot of times it has everything to do with how he "perceives" monogamy and how he was affirmed during his teenage years. "Why Won't He Marry You" will offer freedom to every woman who is still blaming herself for the abandonment or rejection she has experienced in past or current relationships. This is a great read for women who want to understand men a little better. Likewise, I think you will find it is equally a great resource for men who want to understand themselves. Most men who struggle with infidelity and anxiety about marriage really don't know why their mind operates that way. They have grown to accept an existence of being emotionally challenged by monogamy and women have grown to expect it. "Girl, all men are the same.....they are all dogs." You will learn through this literary work that there are some psychological explanations for some of this behavior.

Now nothing is ever truly absolute, but I think you will find my research and spiritual insight very accurate on this matter. I also don't want the reader to feel that these indicators are somehow excuses. We all have a responsibility to make sound decisions and treat the opposite sex with the utmost respect. While that may be the ideal, it is not the norm. If we are honest we must admit that we all make our decisions looking through our own particular lenses. Those lenses come from our own unique experiences and backgrounds. It seems that all of our most profound development happened in our childhood. This is the time when we were most vulnerable, yet also most receptive to instruction. So, as you read this book you will find a creative blend of experiences from childhood all the way through adulthood that in my opinion shape the way the average man thinks. Although these are fictional characters, I am confident that each of you will be able to identify with them in a deep and intimate way. You are about to go on a journey that is filled with emotional peaks and valleys. However, it will allow you to land at a place of deep understanding and breakthrough. This is......"Why He Won't Marry You?"

CHAPTER 1

THE LOCKER ROOM

Somewhere as you are reading this book, there is a group of 12 year old boys that are in the locker room winding down after basketball practice. There are about five of them. There's Johnny the most popular of the group. Then there is Reggie, Tim, Joe, and the least popular tag along William "the church boy." Johnny is tall, handsome, and athletic and all the girls like him. The rest of the boys look up to him as he seems to make everything look cool. One day he stole one of his brother's cigarettes and brought it to school and smoked it in the alley. The rest of the gang was amazed at this taboo act of rebellion. It made him seem like a god. The other guys looked at Johnny as someone who didn't have to follow the rules and did things his way. With every puff, he received more and more admiration from his peers. How cool is this they all nudged each other. "How cool is Johnny" they all cheered. Another day Johnny stole one of his dad's beers from the fridge. During the eight grade school dance, he asked the gang to come to the bathroom with him. He mentioned he had a big surprise. Once in the bathroom, Johnny pulled a beer out of his jacket and everyone's eyes glazed with curiosity. "Wow Johnny....how did you get that?" "What if you get caught?" the gang asked. Johnny, in his normal effortless manner assures the gang that he has everything under control. After earning the gangs acceptance of the idea, he begins to take one sip after another and before you know you it he had drank the whole thing. Johnny then proceeds to brag to the other boys, one day you all will be as cool as me.

Today, Johnny wants to up the ante. He gathers the gang in the locker room after basketball practice and lets them all know that he has something to show them. Johnny proceeds to ask William "the church boy" to be the lookout. As William looks with one eye to see if anyone is coming, he can't help but peek with the other eye to see what is all the fuss about. What could be the next stunt that Johnny would expose the gang to? What could be so important and so secretive that this time we needed a look out? Johnny begins to go in his back pack and pulls out a magazine. William can't make out what the magazine is from the distance, but by the other guys reaction this is something big. This is something really big. What could it be? The anticipation is killing William. He notices that someone is coming so he alarms the guys and he makes a careful mental note of where Johnny hides this infamous magazine. All the guys disperse their different ways to hide their activities. But William is too curious to let the suspense die. He makes an excuse to go to the locker room, and quickly goes directly to the place where he saw Johnny hide the magazine. He finds what he had been looking for. William is totally amazed with what he found. He had never seen a nude woman. But this magazine is full of them. He knows that it's wrong, but he can't help but to keep turning the pages. His anatomy is responding in a way he is not familiar with. His mind is expanded in a way that he is not familiar with. Something is happening on the inside of William, he hates it and he likes it at the same time. William is totally confused. What is this feeling that is coming over me he ponders? Why can't I take my eyes off the pages? William is totally beside himself, not only can he not fully process what he is feeling but he is also torn at what he should do next. Should I tell my parents, or should I protect my friends he asks within himself? He decides that it is not such a big deal and is not worth getting his friends in trouble. The next day, William for some reason has an urge to check and see if Johnny has come back for the magazine and he hasn't.

Alexander J. Patrick

William spends a little more time trying to figure out his new found fascination with the female body. This time he is more comfortable with what he finds and is now beginning to accept this new feeling as positive. Although, there is an innate intuition whispering inside of William letting him know that this is wrong and inappropriate.....it feels so good and now he is not sure how to turn off the images replaying in his mind.

In perfect timing, Johnny walks into the locker with the rest of the guys. William quickly puts the magazine back in its hiding place. William thinks that they will go right for the magazine to pick up where they left off. However, the gang is gathering for another reason today. Johnny has something else he wants to share and he assures the gang this will be the best yet. Johnny says, "Are you guys ready for this?" Everyone eagerly says "yeah Johnny what's up man?" Johnny says "you guys know Susie the girl in our Science class with the long braids?" Everyone nods their head in agreement. Johnny then tells the guys that yesterday "we had sex." Amazed, the whole gang erupts with cheers, and hi-fives! Johnny relishing in his greatest achievement to date, solidifies himself as the big man on campus. All the guys and girls have now heard about Johnny and Susie and the two of them have practically become celebrities in the small inner city Middle School. William "the church boy" finally begins to connect all the dots. He says, it all makes sense now. Look at how Johnny has won everyone's affection. Now, even the girls are admiring him. This is how you gain acceptance. This is what makes you popular. This is why I can't stop looking at this magazine, and why I can't stop thinking about what I saw. Johnny actually got to do what we saw in the magazine. How cool is that? If I can find a girl, to do what Johnny did I will gain acceptance as well. People like him because he was the first to smoke, the first to drink a beer, the first to get a dirty magazine, and now the first to have sex. William says, I want to be good at something. I want to be accepted also. I will go from being the "church boy" to the "cool boy."I will be the new celebrity in the school. After all, why should guys like Johnny be good at everything? Why can't I be popular also? William for the first time has allowed his admiration of Johnny to turn to envy. It's not fair, everybody loves Johnny! Now he has had sex with the prettiest and most popular girl in our grade. Why do I always have to be the tag along that no one notices?

William thinks to himself, how will he process all of these conflicting feelings? He feels that his new found admiration for girls and popularity is what he has been missing. He questions, maybe this is why no one ever noticed me. I have been ignored all this time, because I haven't had sex or even had a desire to. You see, before William saw the magazine he was pretty content with his life. He knew he wasn't the most popular kid, but he accepted that. Coming from a strong Christian home, his parents instilled in him great values like being kind, sharing and always being a good friend. So William never really thought much about being popular or "fitting in" with the crowd. William was never the first one picked to play pick-up games or even to school dances. But up to this point he had been ok with that and was comfortable being the reliable friend that everyone trusted, but not necessarily admired. However, now things seem so different. It feels like he has been deprived and missing out on all the action. All of sudden his life and the way he relates to his friends appears so boring and empty. At the same time, there is a part of him that knows some of the feelings that he has had in the last 24 hours are not right and go against his parents teachings. So as William lies in the bed that night he did not sleep well at all. He tossed and turned all night. He constantly continues to see the images from the magazine flash across his mind and they make him uncomfortably excited. They make his body feel things he is not used to, but since he is at the age of puberty his body is responding. Then there are the cheers and high fives for his friend Johnny. The cheers, the laughter, the affirmation was so exhilarating! It felt so good just to be in the same room when all the guys erupted over the news of Johnny and Susie, William thought.

If it felt that good to us, imagine what it must have felt like for Johnny. William decided he needs to make a choice and he does. That settles it he says, I have made my decision. I am not going to fight these feelings. I want to be affirmed as well. I want to be popular. I want to be noticed.

CHAPTER 2

LEARNING TO HUNT

There are William's all over the world who became womanizers not out of pure desire to be manipulative, but out of necessity to fit in with the pack. The dilemma of wanting acceptance is a powerful and natural instinct. There is an underground hyper sexual culture that starts at a very young age in our schools that promote sexual achievements before academic achievements. The young man that has the most girls is more popular or more "accepted" than the young man with the most academic awards. Therefore, it is common for young men to switch majors of study in high school. They willingly shift from studying math, science, and chemistry to studying girls and how to create "chemistry" with them.

This is what I call learning to hunt. It is identified early on that catching women will yield a prize. And the more you catch the better. So, now as young men we must learn how to hunt. We must learn how to identify our prey. We must learn their vulnerabilities, their tendencies, what they like, what they don't like, and how to present an illusion of attraction to them. This illusion of attraction, is sort of like choosing the right bait. When you put cheese on a mouse trap, the mouse smells the cheese and follows it. The young man's job is to make the cheese smell so good that the mouse will ignore the trap. The desire for the cheese or bait of choice becomes stronger than the possibility of being trapped. What is her cheese? What type of cologne does she like? What makes her laugh? Does she like flowers, or does she like candy? Which one of her friends will be the best mouth piece for me? Once the mouse gets close enough to the cheese, the trap will be set. Yes, this sounds barbaric and very insensitive. But we must remember, this young man is fighting for relevance, acceptance, and popularity. At this stage of his life, he has no conception of hurting someone's feelings or the long term damage his actions may cause.

William now sets out to be a student of how to become accepted by his peers. His primary objective is to learn how to select the right bait to get the right girl, so that he can ultimately be affirmed and get the recognition he so desperately desires. He has learned by observing some of the most popular guys in school that girls like three very important things. Girls like guys who are good at sports, dress nice and have a sense of humor. William already knew he wasn't good at sports and he was very introverted or shy. The only area he saw that he could compete in was he would need to become the absolute best dressed kid in middle school. All summer, he read magazines and watched music videos to try to figure out what are all the latest fashions and what would get the girls attention. He even created his own business cutting his neighbors yards to earn extra money for shoes and clothes. You see, up to this point William has basically only worn what most would consider church clothes to school. He was always neat and presentable, but not very fashionable. It's the summer before his first year of high school and he is determined to have the most impressive wardrobe. He had earned an extra $500 over the summer and he saved every penny and planned to put it all towards school clothes. His parents were very inquisitive. They had never seen this side of their son. Past summers, they had bought all of Williams clothes and any extra money that he earned he would spend on comic books or video games. In the past, they would do all of his shopping at JC Penny and Sears. This year William refused to step foot in either of those stores. It was a strange transition, but his parents ultimately found peace in the fact that their son had worked so hard this summer and had earned his own money to do the majority of his own shopping. Little did they know, this school year, these new clothes and all the new attention that is about to come his way will be a pivotal moment in this young man's life. His parents will ask the question several years later, what happened….how did he get so far off track. The answer is the summer before the ninth grade.

William was sure he picked just the right outfits to gain an advantage on all the other guys. He was determined to be noticed and get an opportunity to get the girls just like Johnny did last year. On the first day of school William even snuck in his father's closet and splashed on some of his favorite cologne. He noticed his dad would put it on for special occasions or when he wanted to impress his mom. So he had it all together. The right clothes, the right cologne, fresh kicks (shoes), haircut, everything is working and he is feeling like a million dollars. He goes into his first class and he scans the room to see who he will put the moves on. Only thing is, before he could pick his victim he feels a tap on his shoulder. It's Susie the most popular girl from last year. She ask him, are those the new Jordan's? This is the moment William has been dreaming about. This is the moment he has been playing in his head over and over again. Inside himself, he screams "YES!!!!!!!" "It worked!!!!!!" But wait, I still haven't responded to her he remembers. He looks her in her hazel eyes and is totally frozen. In his mind, he is thinking man she looks so good. This is the moment you have been waiting for dummy. SAY SOMETHING!!!! He is frozen, and remembers that he put so much effort into dressing that he never actually figured he would have to talk to the girls. Susie, irritably says "are you ok?" William still cannot gather the nerve to respond. Susie finally walks away and whispers to her girlfriend what's wrong with him? William is totally embarrassed and can't believe he just blew the opportunity of a lifetime. The rest of the day William can't focus on his studies, he had everything perfect and then froze at his moment of truth. Distraught and frustrated when he gets home that evening he goes straight to his room and gets in bed. When his mom gets home, she comes in his room and asks "what's wrong Willy?" That's what his mom calls him for short. She says usually around this time you are playing your video games or practicing your drums for church on Sunday. William too embarrassed to tell his mom what happened decides to instead change the subject. He comes out from under the covers and looks at his mom and says can I ask you a question? His mom, says with deep endearment "sure anything Willy." He ask, "what made you like dad?" William's mother paused and thought to herself this is an odd question. She proceeded hoping that it would make her son feel better. She said to him, son I liked your father because he made me comfortable and I felt safe when I was with him. William perked up in his bed visibly intrigued. But how did he do that William asked. She said, he just was really good at being himself. He wasn't trying to be anything that wasn't naturally God given to him. So nothing was ever forced. Your father was "smooooothe" she chuckled and blushed a little. William jumped out of bed and hugged his mom with the biggest hug she had felt in a while. That's it he says, I just have to be myself. He scans over his life experiences and personality traits and tries to come to a nucleus of understanding of who he is. He goes through his own personal litmus test, trying to identify when do I feel the most in control? When do I feel the most calm and confident? Was it at church? Not really. What about when I play video games? Not so much. Wait, I remember! I think I've got it William said. He remembered the experience he had with Johnny's magazine. He remembered, how there were so many beautiful women and he needed to somehow not put them on such a high pedestal. I just need to relax and not take them so seriously. So he came up with a strategy, that he wouldn't be picky. That any girl would suffice. Whichever, girl I can be comfortable with is who I will pursue? That's it; I'll practice with as many girls that will give me attention.

Because he wore all the right clothes and smelled really good, he continued to get attention and got more and more comfortable talking to girls. What started out as a hobby to gain friends, has now become almost addictive. He now has graduated from sneaking a peak at his friend's dirty magazines, to now he has his own collection. After all, this is some of his hunting training material. What once was something optional, is now a strong growing desire for more and more female attention. His wardrobe continues to get better and better. His confidence is growing and now some of the guys who looked at him as the tag along are now interested in being his tag along. William has gotten in a good flow. Some time has passed and he is now a senior in high school. He has even had sex a few times. He really didn't know what he was doing, but he knew it would get him some cool points to at least pretend. The sex was never really what he was after. He only wanted to recreate that moment in the locker room when all of his friends where so affirming of Johnny. He wanted that feeling. He really wanted to be Johnny.

<u>With each female capture, the prize is a cultural embrace that is the most addictive of all.</u> Even the friends of the Williams "victims" are now curious. They snicker and blush when he walks by after one of them shares her story of her experience with him. The others immediately begin to secretly plot how they can be next. There is now a never ending stream of attention, phone calls, text, and constant

affirmation. Even the girls that call him a "dog" will secretly wink at him when her other friends aren't looking. The Williams' of the world are now hooked. He has it made. No one has really taught him about the negative consequences of his actions and to date he has not faced any. It has been all good, ever since that day in the locker room when he saw that dirty magazine. He is now fixated on the ability to make girls feel good, which in turn seemingly gives him an advantage in life. An advantage he couldn't get with good grades, an advantage he couldn't gain in sports, nor could he gain in being a good Christian. Nothing got him the stares and whispers of admiration that he got from being a skilled hunter of the opposite sex.

Most adult women who are frustrated with a man who won't commit, was at some point a teenage girl fascinated by a boy who dated several girls at once. You see, this mindset is not just one sided. It is not solely about a young man becoming popular. It's about what young women find attractive. The good student with good manners and has great potential was not usually the one that the girls liked. As a matter a fact, in most schools this guy was not even voted most likely to succeed. If we are honest, we all grew up in a culture where popularity is the goal and popularity defines attractiveness on many levels. If we can agree on this, then the only thing left to agree on is what would make a young man or young woman popular? Traditionally, for young men the alpha male dominant characteristics start with how they relate to the opposite sex. Unfortunately, during this phase of learning for young men there is no incentive for being considerate, polite, or even honest. The truth is that these behaviors and habits could be easily be redirected by redirecting how popularity is determined at a young age. Again, most of the women that don't understand the adult male culture of infidelity once participated in a youth culture of celebrating it. Now I really need to highlight the fact, that this portion of the book is not a blame game and definitely not an attempt to defend poor decision making but merely a diagnosis. No one is to blame for the ideology most men have around commitment. If anything the blame lands on the youth culture of acceptance and popularity that exploits the curiosity of young minds and plants permanent seeds of lust and dishonesty for a temporary moment of void gratification.

Let's think about it for a minute. We all adjust our mindsets and behaviors to whatever the system of reward is in any particular culture. Regardless of the culture, we quickly assess what the system of reward is and then we must make adjustments to solve the demand for the current method of compliance. This truly is a method of survival more than a method of preference "at the time." If I were to do a random anonymous survey of individuals who have fallen into infidelity, substance abuse, and even alcoholism. I believe I could prove this theory with actual data based on the responses. The questions I would ask, would trace back to the first encounter with that act of dysfunction. <u>I believe the data would teach us that most bad habits, start with a simple desire to be affirmed, or a complex desire to cope with the pain of not being affirmed.</u>

Did you know that some Neurologist suggest that the part of the brain that responds to not being accepted, is the same part of the brain that responds to physical pain? This suggest that not being accepted or "how we are accepted" plays a vital role in how we process things. I mean who wants to feel physical pain? When you have a tooth ache, you immediately go to the dentist. When you have a headache, you immediately take some aspirin. Likewise, when we are not accepted we will do whatever it takes to fit in and become a part of a group. Think back to your childhood. Wasn't there at least one time that you "faked it?" What I mean by this, is that you saw a group of kids doing some behavior or activity that you genuinely had no interest in. However, you pretended to be in the know and proceeded to mimic the activity or behavior to the best of your ability hoping no one would notice that you were a novice. Yes you have! I know you have! We all have! That is the power of wanting to be accepted. It causes you to take on behaviors that don't necessarily reflect your values. <u>The issue is if you are not careful when you become accepted because of a behavior that doesn't reflect who you are, you have to continue the behavior to maintain your acceptance. Sooner or later, what you did to fit in has now become what you do to survive. Then what you do to survive has now become who you are.</u>

This actually is such a broad concept that it fits just about any mold of understanding for behavior. If you find kids who are in gangs, you will find other kids who affirmed the gang to them. You will find a group of kids who planted seeds about the gang to each other and how being a part will make them accepted and essentially loved and respected by their peers. Once a part of the gang, you must become good at the activities associated with the system of affirmation for gangs. There is fighting, stealing, selling drugs, and whatever activity determines that you will get the applause and kudos from your comrades. No matter how dysfunctional the behavior is, it all traces back to the desire to be good at the things that make people notice you. You find the same psychology with kids who are heavily involved in athletics. I would argue that the thing that made them practice to get better was someone affirming them. The first time they made a basketball shot or ran a touchdown and their parents or their peers began to clap with amazement was the moment it all made sense. That was the moment they decided to get better, because this "act" makes people accept me.

For the woman who is reading this that has blamed herself for her man's infidelity or lack of desire to get married. I want you to know that his anxiety around marriage or settling down likely has nothing to do with you or the relationship. It is not that you are not attractive enough and it is not that you are not marriage material. In most cases you are not competing with other women. You are competing with a teenage boy in a middle school locker room that never mentally transitioned to manhood. You are in a lot of cases competing with a man who understands all of his vitality in the past tense. The reason why most men are apprehensive of marriage is because they cannot relate marriage to affirmation and acceptance in manhood. In his mind, the moment he embraces marriage he simultaneously embraces an empty existence. There is no more hunting, no more pursuit, no more competition, no more popularity and quite frankly no more alpha male ego stroking. For the past 15-25 years he has studied and mastered a certain system that strokes his alpha male ego and allows him to be "the man." Marriage will bring all this to a screeching halt. Where will the admiration come from as a married man? How will he now solve the desire to hunt, when marriage suggest hunting is now illegal?

CHAPTER 3

CATCH AND RELEASE

In hunting and fishing terms, there is a term called "catch and release." This is when a skilled hunter is no longer hunting for food or survival. But merely hunting for the sport or competition. Typically, a skilled fisherman puts his catch into three categories.

Fish you throw back: This is a fish that is fun to catch. There is great enjoyment in learning how to hunt or fish. Most avid hunters or fisherman will tell you that it can be one of the most relaxing sports. In some cases, a fisherman can spend the entire day fishing and throw most of his catch back. Now, this can be for various reasons. The primary reason that a fisherman throws back a fish is because it is too small or the manner that the fish was caught indicates it may not be good to eat. Remember this, as it will be a good note to reference later. <u>Fish that you throw back can be caught usually with cheap bait because they will eat just about anything.</u>

Fish you eat: This fish is equally fun to catch, but you are going to need to put a little more thought into the type of bait that you use. Also, important to note this fish is a little harder to pull in and is likely to put up a fight. Well, in the life of a fisherman this makes the catch that much more rewarding. This particular fish is just the right size and makes for a good dinner.

Trophy Fish: This fish is rare and very difficult to catch. A fisherman has to go to extreme lengths to capture a trophy fish. They have to venture to the coldest and deepest of waters, and use the most creative of baits. However, this fish when caught is not eaten nor is it thrown back. This fish is for showing of and boasting. In a lot of cases this fish is memorialized and kept to show everyone how skilled of a hunter/fisherman he is.

Now someone reading this is wondering, that is very informative but what does it have to do with marriage or monogamy. Well, it actually has everything to do with it. See, I already mentioned that William became a student of girls in middle school. He learned what type of bait he needed to catch the girls so that he could be affirmed. What he also learned that I have not mentioned yet, is that different bait catch different types of girls. And just like a fisherman put their catch in different categories, so did William learn how to put young ladies in categories.

When William got old enough and his parents knew that he was dating girls, etc. He learned very early what types of girls his family and friends would approve of (trophy fish) or what type of girls he basically needed to keep a secret (throw-back fish). Young men always want to be affirmed for having a trophy. Sometimes the love of the hunt will cause you to end up with some fish that you know you really need to throw back. For the women reading this book, make sure you are not a (throw-back fish). This is not a good place to be in and I can tell you exactly how you know if this is you.

If you are a throw-back fish you are mainly kept a secret. You will be caught but not kept. Your emotions and time will be utilized but you will never stay in the boat with him for very long. You are meant to be part of the game and not part of his life. Someone reading this is saying that sounds so harsh. Truth is, there are a lot of women who enjoy being the throw-back fish. They don't mind the late night visits and minimal commitment. Why you may ask? Women are equally looking to fill a void of affirmation in their lives. So even if it is only for an hour or two at 2am, it still is affirming and comforting to know she is in demand. It still solves an immediate need she has and helps her to feel good about herself. Someone wants me, even if it is just for my body I am still "wanted" and "accepted." This is the result of our bodies being touched too soon, and our minds left unattended. This is a result of an eroding culture of highly sexual, yet shallow individuals who again just need the next high. No matter what the long term cost may be. We just want our needs met. No matter if a child is produced with someone you are not married too or have any real commitment to. No matter if more than 70% of the relationship is abusive and dysfunctional. No matter if we are aware that other relationships exist because second or third place is better than no place at all. Please don't feel guilty or bad if this sounds like an experience you have found yourself in. Truthfully, I think we all have been in this place at one time or another. Some of us thought we were in actual relationships, only to find out later we were a throw-back fish. It is not your fault. We are trapped in a society where men fish for women they don't necessarily plan to keep, and women don't necessarily demand to be kept.

If you are a fish that is kept, then you are likely in the sweet spot. This is the girl that is usually identified as the "main chic." See how lost we are, there are even cultural terms that permit men to have a main chick, and possibly a "side chic?" At any rate, the fish that is kept is usually smart, attractive and trustworthy. She has all the characteristics of a wife. She comes from a balanced upbringing and has great morals. As I mentioned earlier, the "keeper" fish will usually put up a little more fight before you can reel them in. She is not prone to games and manipulation. She plays hard to get and knows what she wants. She has been mentored and taught what is right, wrong, acceptable and unacceptable. However, the William's of the world love this kind of challenge. He pulls out all the stops until he gets her attention and causes her to take him seriously. The only problem is that he doesn't even take himself seriously. This is still very much a game to him and he has no concept of what type of value a young lady of this caliber has. She will eventually fall for him and he will eventually mistreat her. She has everything he needs, but not everything he wants. He won't learn until later, that this will be one of his greatest regrets. However, the regret will begin the correction of his thinking and begin the self-inspection that he so desperately needs. Truth is, for a young man like William there is nothing the "keeper" could do to make him love her exclusively. He has only decided to partially keep her because even in his immaturity he recognizes her greatness. While he is not ready to fully commit to her, he definitely wants to take her off the market so no one else can have her. One day he will slow down and he wants to have someone to fall back on and his belief is that she will be there. This is the ideal woman staring him in the face, but he won't realize this until it is likely much too late.

The trophy is a lot more complicated. This particular young lady has several different personalities you may engage. She is extremely beautiful, and "she knows it." All her life she has been told how pretty she is and everyone always wanted to get to know her. The girls hate her, and the boys love her. She was always the most popular in high school. She was the equivalent of Johnny. She was captain of the cheerleading team, and first one to get a car. She had the red Honda Accord, with the sunroof and rims. You all remember that right? Her attractiveness and popularity has either defined her, or made her ironically insecure. She does not need to be trustworthy because she has always been affirmed because of her looks and nice clothes. She will only date guys that will add to her popularity or can somehow match her level of "awesomeness." This is usually the one that guys like William fall for. However, she is really the only one that can humble William and make his palms sweat. She is the only one that can make him fumble at his words and lose his smooth, calm and cool persona. Remember his experience the first day of high school. You guys remember Susie, yeah Susie was the trophy. On the first day of high school she made him forget how to put a sentence together and she still has that effect. If William was smarter, he would know that the trophy is not always the best. Trophies indicate competition and competing is not really what you want when it comes to relationships. If you have to constantly compete for someone's attention and affection then the relationship is likely unsustainable. The trophy is amazing when and if you can catch one. However, chances are that everyone is competing for the trophy. If her moral compass is not in the right place you will not be able to keep her attention. "If" she has allowed all the attention, affirmation and applause over the years to define her, she will likely become a dominant alpha-female who cannot be satisfied by one man. Likewise she will be chasing her next high which is not likely solved by guys like William.

Let me continue to explain through the vicarious college years of William. Through all of this, William was a pretty good student. He didn't really pick up too many bad habits, except being a womanizer. So he was able to get into college about an hour from his home. This was great because it was just far enough to have his freedom, but close enough to stay in contact with some of his "friends" and continue to attend his church with his parents. His sophomore year he has a girlfriend. Let's call her Rebecca. Now Rebecca, like William came from a Christian home. She was beautiful and very smart. She was what William would consider a "keeper" fish but not necessarily a trophy. He really cared for her deeply and his parents loved her. Rebecca had become like part of the family. She was very much like William in that she was mostly quiet and stayed to herself. She was very clear about what she wanted to do with her life and would not entertain any foolishness. William really liked that about her. This is the one everyone would think that William would end up marrying one day. They seemed to be so right for each other. However, there was one problem. He had learned to love the hunt. The one thing that Rebecca could not offer him was the adrenaline of the hunt. She could not curb that desire to be affirmed by his boys and considered "the man" because of how good of a hunter he was. He loved hunting so much that he willingly entertained some throw-backs just for the sport of it. He knew a throw-back would never meet his parents or his friends. The throw-back serves only one purpose. To quench the desire of the hunt and stroke the ego of an alpha-male who cannot understand monogamy. He cannot understand it because his societal culture offers no affirmation connected to it. He has several throw backs, and has not learned yet the consequences of these actions. He is still focused on the hunt and most of his actions are selfish in nature.

Now it's also interesting to note that while he has a great girlfriend that really is all that he needs and more. He still has a void for a trophy fish. He still is not totally satisfied. Is it because Rebecca is not attractive enough? Is it because she doesn't dress nice enough? What could it be? It's actually none of those things. <u>The thing I want the men reading to learn is that while William spent so much of his youth learning how to bait women, he never realized that the whole time he was the one being baited.</u> William never realized that while yes he has become a master of baiting young ladies, he didn't have the self-awareness to understand that from the moment he looked at Johnny's magazine he was actually the one being baited. He was literally hooked from the moment he heard the applause and cheers when his friends learned that Johnny and Susie had sex. He was attracted to the way his friends reacted to the news of Johnny's successful venture of pre-marital sex. This was his cheese and he was the mouse drawn and hypnotized by the smell. He was drawn to the look of satisfaction and accomplishment Johnny had on his face. There was a seed planted in him on that day. This seed was later nourished and watered for many years thereafter. This seed I am referring to is lust. Not just lust for the opposite sex. Lust for attention and lust for acceptance. He would not learn until many years into his adulthood that lust cannot ever be satisfied or quenched. He wanted a trophy not because he needed it, he wanted a trophy simply because he felt like it would escalate his persona. His perception told him, yes Rebecca is great but what I want is a young woman that will turn all the heads on campus. You see it was never about what the young lady had to offer, it was always about how can being with her gratify my reputation and image with my peers. William doesn't know it but he is still stuck in the middle school locker room mentally and says to himself, I want that feeling again. I want the feeling from the middle school locker room. Well, the truth is William will be chasing this feeling for many more years because it was never real. It was an illusion. It was a moment created to distract him from his destiny and plant seeds of lust and instability in his spirit. That one moment would ensure that he would become a dishonest, disloyal, womanizer who could never be satisfied. That one moment would allow him to be polished and well put together on the outside, but filthy and restless on the inside. He is restless because the applause is never enough. The affirmation from his peers will never be enough. This desire just grows and grows and grows into an empty oblivion. Look at most famous musicians, artist and actors and how their lives typically play out. They have everything at their disposal. They have all the money one person could spend in ten lifetimes. They have large homes, fancy cars, and people surrounding them all the time. However, most of them spend most of their lives chasing the next high from substances such as drugs and alcohol. Most of them have been married numerous times and have children all over the nation. Most of them don't have many authentic relationships, but mainly employees posing as friends to stroke their egos and make them feel good about themselves. When it's all said and done, most of them have the similar testimony that none of the money, fame or applause could produce happiness. Most of them would describe it as more of an addiction that was unhealthy and led to a great disconnect from anyone who genuinely loved them. The love of applause and affirmation that is not connected to genuine love is a trap that leads to an unhealthy mindset that is never quite satisfied or at peace. I would argue that most of these high profile entertainers suffer from the same mental disease that causes the average man to be unsettled with one woman. They are chasing the next high, instead of chasing what's real and secure.

CHAPTER 4

THE WAKE-UP CALL

It's now senior year of college and Rebecca decided to end her relationship with William. She has had enough of hearing about all his dishonesty and dealing with the games he seems to be playing. She no longer desires to be in "waiting" for him to get himself together. She has had enough and lets him know that she will not continue to be his door mat. William with his calm, cool, collective self doesn't panic one bit. After all, he has not had a lonely night since his sophomore year of high school. He has plenty of female attention and figures that Rebecca will come to her senses sooner or later. It's time for the senior banquet and everyone is picking their dates. William being the playboy that he is decides to go alone. He didn't have a trophy at the present time and he definitely wouldn't bring one of his throw-backs. He decided he would just come alone and hang with his boys until someone caught his attention. As always, William shows up dressed in all the latest fashion. He is what the older people call "casket sharp." He walks in the room with the utmost confidence. Patrolling the scene and looking for who all is in attendance. He spots a few of his boys and they begin to converse. One of his friends says, "man look at Sheila she sure is looking good tonight." His other friend speaks up, "yeah she looks good but she has nothing on Jessica." Then one of them says to William "who do you have your eye on?" William begins to scan the room again like an eagle looking for its prey. While scanning the room he notices a crowd forming in the lobby. He asks his friends "what's going on in the lobby?" William is too cool to go see for himself, so he stays back and just continues to wonder. The crowd is growing larger and larger and he even sees a few people taking pictures. Now his ego is starting to take a little hit, because he is used to being the center of attention. He sees the crowd begin to break up a little and finally he sees two familiar faces walk into the ballroom. Wait, is that Rebecca? It's his ex-girlfriend and she looks amazing! However, who is the guy she is with and why is everyone acting so star struck? Wait, he looks familiar also. No, it can't be? William wipes his eyes to get a closer look. You have to be kidding me he says to himself. It's Johnny his old childhood friend. Johnny was the most popular guy in middle school and high school. He was the first one of us to have sex and had even more girls than William. As a matter fact, it was from watching Johnny that William figured out how to get noticed and gain popularity with the girls. Well, Johnny was a football star in high school and got a scholarship to a major university about an hour away from the school William and Rebecca went to. The word on the street is he is about to be drafted into the NFL and is about to be a millionaire. People are saying that he has already bought his parents another house and he has a brand new Mercedes. But why is he here and most importantly why is he with Rebecca, William asks? William is having trouble processing what he is feeling. He has so many internal conflicts going on at once. The first emotion he feels is regret. Rebecca somehow looks different. She looks so beautiful and happy. Her hair is just right and her dress is out of this world. Wow! How did I let her get away? The next emotion he feels is competitive. How does Johnny feel that he can just take my girl? I don't care that he is some big football star. He says within himself, that's my girl! She will always be my girl! The last and most profound emotion that he feels is concern. I wonder if he is treating her right, he ponders? He is thinking, I know this guy and he has more girls than me. He can't possibly treat her the way she needs to be treated. She can do so much better than him. Rebecca deserves better, he says.

William comes up with a strategy. He decides he needs to talk to her. How can I get her alone says William? He waits until Johnny is distracted with all the groupies trying to get autographs and gestures Rebecca to meet him by the punch bowl. She obliges and heads in his direction. William asks her, "what are you doing here with him?" Rebecca responds "what do you mean William?" He responds, "why would you come here with him? First of all you knew I would be here and of all the people you could bring you bring my childhood friend?" Rebecca is confused at William's response and lets him know that Johnny is a very nice guy and she will not apologize for being with him. Rebecca stares at William directly in his eyes with a look of deep sincerity and says words that would ring in Williams head and heart for years to come. "If you really cared about me it wouldn't have taken me coming with Johnny for you to really notice me." She then takes a deep breath looks over at Johnny signing autographs and says very intently "GOOD-BYE WILLIAM!" She turns and walks away back in the direction of Johnny. "Wait.....Rebecca let me explain" William says. She does not turn around and acts as if she doesn't hear him. This is first time William can remember that he is totally rejected and he cannot smooth talk his way out of it. He feels weak and helpless. He decides to leave the party.

He immediately comes up with a plan. I know what I can do. I need to erase this night from my memory. I will call one of my throw-backs and they will keep me company. He calls one, no answer. He calls another, no answer. He calls a third, his "go-to" when he needs some time to clear his head. Let's call her Katie. Katie answers, as she always does but there is a great commotion in the background. "What's up William" she says? "I was wondering if you wanted to hang out," says William. Her reply cut like a knife in his back. Katie says, "I can't tonight. Didn't you hear Johnny the future NFL draft pick is on campus and there is about to be an after party?" Katie says, "I wouldn't miss it for the world." But wait William says, "I figured we could watch a movie and just..... you know." Katie obviously distracted, eventually says "William I really have to go. Give me a call next week or something." WOW!!! I can't believe this William mutters under his breath. Lastly, he calls Rebecca maybe she has gotten away from Johnny and will give him a few minutes to explain himself. She doesn't answer. He calls again, she doesn't answer. His pride won't allow him to leave a message. He finally has to face the facts. Tonight, he is forced to confront all the emotions he is feeling. Tonight, he will have to ask himself tough questions and he has no false affirmation to dull the pain. This is a place he has never been in. It's either he go to the party and watch everyone drool over Rebecca and Johnny or just go back to his room and be alone. Eventually, he had to accept the fact that there was no avoiding the next twenty-four hours of reflection. He decided not to go to the after party. He just sat in his room and stared at the ceiling. He would not sleep a wink all night. By his actions and past decisions he had allowed himself to be sentenced to a mental prison. His sentence was regret, a deflated ego and concern for what was possibly the girl of his dreams.

His regret comes from the fact that all of a sudden feelings that he didn't know he had begun to surface. All of a sudden, he felt like Rebecca was supposed to be with him. In just a few short hours, he had appreciated her more than all the years they dated. William is not quite mature enough yet to realize that these emotions he is feeling are really not authentic. You see, sometimes as men the woman you have looks mediocre to you until she is on the arm of another man. It is again deeply rooted in the psychology of manhood, competition and wanting to be affirmed. There is nothing more emasculating than for another man to take your lady. Better yet, you willingly let her go and she becomes someone else's prize. The same is true for women as well. However, this feeling is not genuine love. <u>Many people go through great lengths to convince their exes to give them another try and they really never loved them in first place. By the mere fact</u>

42

that they couldn't stand to see them with someone else, they convinced themselves that they could not live without the person. When in reality, they just could not live with rejection. It can be intimidating to know that a new relationship may erase your memory, and may eliminate your access. Remember, we always want to be accepted and affirmed.

His ego is also deflated. Johnny came and completely shut the entire campus down. He also has Williams girl on his arm. You see, an inflated ego often times allows us to not deal with real emotion. As long as we feel like we are hot stuff and everybody embraces that idea, we never really have to take accountability for being rude, inconsiderate, dishonest, disloyal, or any other negative characteristic. Ego drives poor behavior because it allows you to create a persona that only has to take itself into consideration. That's why you hear really egocentric entertainers refer to themselves in the third person. It's because that personality or alter ego only has to consider maintaining its image or brand. Sadly, people love it regardless of how low the morals are associated with that alter ego. If you don't believe me, take a look at the ratings of some of the reality T.V. shows that mainly dramatize relationships that are filled with contention and strife. However, when someone's ego is deflated they become a regular human being that is held accountable for their actions just like everyone else. For the first time in a long time William has to be accountable for his actions. He has to look at the role he played in all of this. He begins thinking to himself, why did I take Rebecca for granted? What did she do to deserve me being dishonest? How in the world could I not appreciate such a great person? He then asks himself the most profound question during his mental prison sentence? Was it all worth it? All of his "throw-backs" really had no real investment in him nor did he in them. So when he really needed them, especially on a night like tonight they were not there. He would have thought that when he spoke with Katie on the phone that she would have heard the desperation in his voice. The others that he called saw his number on the caller id at such a late hour and didn't pick up. There was simply no investment there and no sense of urgency to come to Williams rescue. They were only having fun and enjoying the hunt. There was no time for serious matters, substantial feelings, or providing resolution to any real conflict. That is not a part of the equation of a relationship with a throw-back.

Now to think about it Rebecca was the only one that really had my back William ponders. He is now going through his mental rolodex and reflecting on all the relationships of his past. Most of them led to a dead end and provided no real benefit. All of the hunting he had done over the years came crashing down in one night. In this short window of time he is looking at the truth about relationships and the value they add. He comes to the truth that real relationships are not about quantity but about quality. He had spent so much time trying to be everything to everyone. He had spent so much energy trying to please everyone and trying to ensure that everyone liked him. Tonight he learned that in reality, all that matters is that the people that really matter like you. This was a hard lesson for William to digest, but he could no longer run from the truth. He began to have flashbacks of the time when his grandfather was diagnosed with cancer. Rebecca stayed up all night with him while they drove 6 hours to his hospital bed. Not to mention, this one time when he was about to fail chemistry Rebecca tutored him until he got a passing grade. Since Rebecca was from out of town, every Sunday she went home with him to church and had dinner with his family. She even taught his little sister how to ride a bike. Now to think of it, Rebecca was like family William said to himself. She was perfect and I blew it, he says to himself.

Now after having this moment of clarity, he has to deal with the reality of what he left her vulnerable to. Now because he did not appreciate her, she is involved with Johnny the ultimate ladies' man. Has Johnny changed? Is he treating her right? What are they doing right now, William wonders? Sure, he is about to be rich. Sure, he's tall, athletic and good looking. But that doesn't mean she is happy,

William ponders. Then a question seemed to come out of the sky and hit William like a ton of bricks. It was almost audible and loud within his conscious. He imagined this must be what the voice of God sounds like. He heard "Was she safer being with you?" William was totally humbled. It was as if all of a sudden all of his dishonest ways began to flash before his mind at once. It was true, how can I be jealous and concerned when I treated Rebecca so horribly when we were together. As a matter of fact, if I hadn't seen her with Johnny tonight I probably would not even be thinking about her. What a horrible person I am, William reflects. He finally began to embrace the idea that the way he had been living was not worth the hurt and pain it has caused. But now that he has had this epiphany, what does he do? How does he change? It is one thing to hear the alarm clock, and it's another thing to actually get out of bed. William's biggest challenge now is how do I change? Where do I even begin to try to be a new person? He had never been in a relationship with just one person and honestly was petrified of it. What if things don't work, and I don't have anything or anyone to fall back on? What if I am honest and completely transparent and it backfires on me? The thing William is most afraid of is being vulnerable. He feels that having just one relationship is too much power for one young lady to have over him. Being with one person doesn't allow him to use his ego as his strength. A young man is used to being in control and he subconsciously feels monogamy will make him weak. Guys like William do not usually learn until much later in life how to balance monogamy and strength of character. For most men, we find our strength in collecting things. <u>Bragging rights is the right of passage into manhood.</u> The more of anything you have, the more cool points you get. The more pair of Jordan's you have the more confidence you have. The more girls you have as a teenager, the more confidence you have. As an adult man, the more houses, cars, tailor made suits, and etc. the more confidence you possess. A man must learn to turn this switch off as an adult as it relates to women. It takes years to master, and is the breeding ground for infidelity and anxiety concerning marriage. The question most adult men ask themselves is how can one woman satisfy my desire to hunt and be affirmed as an alpha male? By definition, only having one of anything is not equivalent to the alpha male. The alpha male dominates and rules a certain territory. His ego is constantly stroked and respect is freely given. This is what most men at their core yearn for, and finding it within marriage or a monogamous relationship is difficult to obtain.

Now here is what is even more complex. Teenagers who learn how to hunt and become good at it also become sexually active. In regards to sex as a teenager, most don't even have the capacity to understand the life-long consequences of their actions. Having sex for most youth is a part of the system of reward. Therefore, young men learn how to hunt for young ladies because it is one of the most natural ways to be affirmed by their peers. When you combine puberty and all of the body's natural responses from male and females it is a match made in heaven, but meant for destruction. That will make sense later. The activities associated with hunting are very addictive. Pre-marital sex is probably one of the strongest bondages to a young man or woman who is attempting to live a virtuous life. Once you open Pandora's box, there is no way to close it. What was done out of a naïve desire for acceptance is now a legitimate strong hold in your life. In Williams's case, sex with girls started as a want so he could have some bragging stories for the locker room. However, as he got into college it became a need. Sex became something that had taken over his mind. Other than his school work, it's really all he wanted to do. Him and his boys would just talk to girls and see how long it would take to have sex with them. They would even place bets on who could sleep with a girl the fastest. This behavior became a way of life for William and his friends.

Now take into consideration that William has now decided to change his life. William has had his first real heartbreak and he is humbled for the first time in his life. He is vulnerable and ready to change. There is only one problem. Just because you learn to hate your past, doesn't mean you immediately forget it. William desires a new life, but is still stuck with some old habits. Change is not something that just takes place because you desire it. <u>Change takes place when the change in your mind is matched with a change of your habits.</u> Because William doesn't understand this quite yet he will have many relapses over the next few years. One thing is for sure, a seed of change has been planted and he wants to do better. His eyes have been opened to the potential of a better life. He is not quite sure how he can make the adjustment, but he is definitely willing to try.

CHAPTER 5

THE ALPHA-FEMALE

Now Rebecca, has graduated from college and is doing quite well for herself. She has landed a good job, and is very active in her local church. She is single and hasn't really dated anyone since her and Johnny split up about 3 years ago. Williams, suspicions were right and although she liked Johnny very much the relationship fell apart the moment he became a professional football player. He was drafted in the first round and his life changed overnight. He had groupies in every city and although Rebecca really wanted it to work, she realized she could not endure another relationship riddled with deceit and lies. However, when this relationship ended she became bitter. You see, Rebecca and many women like her felt like if I did everything right.....good grades, don't sleep around, go to church, and be loyal that she would be affirmed also. The

Rebecca's of the world feel that if I give honesty, it will be reciprocated. If I give loyalty, it will be reciprocated. In a lot of cases those expectations are not met and it makes women like Rebecca guarded and bitter. It causes them to take on a role I like to call the Alpha-Female.

Alpha Female —The alpha female is defined as the most dominant, powerful, or assertive woman in a particular group. The alpha female is not very emotional because honestly there is no room for emotion in the heat of competition. The alpha female is confident, competitive and focuses on being the best in class in everything she is associated with. She is often a collector and enjoys options. She does not like to be boxed in or made to feel vulnerable under any circumstances. The alpha female characteristics come from a unique blend of genetics, experiences, and especially rejection.

I have noticed that many single females have taken on these traits. A woman being betrayed while exhibiting softness and gentleness will cause her to create an alter ego that is hard and tough like leather. You see in most cases the way the cycle goes is by the time most men are trying to shed their alter ego, women are working on creating theirs. Because they were vulnerable at one point in their life and were hurt, mistreated, cheated on and lied too. They now have decided to become hard. The Alpha Female says to herself, I will not be hurt again. I will not be vulnerable again.

I will develop a shell that cannot be penetrated by anyone. I will create an existence that is career focused, and I will use men only for entertainment purposes. After all, exposing your feelings and caring for someone will only get you hurt in the long run. So she has created a new identity with a new attitude. This attitude is not necessarily natural for most women, but can be easily taught or built as a defense mechanism. I believe most women will naturally lean to be nurturing and trusting when in an environment she feels allows it. I think at a women's core she wants to feel delicate, protected and safe. She will only take on the Alpha Female role as a reaction to the life that is presented to her. She is not naturally bitter, battered and broken. You must remember she has a series of experiences that have shaped her way of thinking. If she is defensive, it is likely because her trust was abused. If she is cold, it's likely because her warmth was ignored. If she is bitter, it's likely because being sweet offered no advancement. When a man meets an Alpha Female he must be very careful to not engage her past. He must make every attempt to ignite her future.

Again, we all are just looking to be affirmed, survive, and thrive by any means necessary. The standard way of thinking for this woman is, I do not need a man. As stated earlier, the Alpha Female is not a permanent disposition but a defense mechanism. She really wants to release all of her fears and anxiety to a man that can say "I got you" and she knows he means it. However, she can't stand to be hurt again so she plays it safe. She rejects the idea of submission, not because she doesn't desire it. She rejects submission because it's not available. So she attempts to block out the idea of a meaningful relationship and she goes to brunch with her best girlfriend on Sunday once a month. She has put herself on the fast track at the Fortune 500 Company she works for. She is already the youngest executive on the leadership team. She is focused on her health, nutrition and her spirituality but that is about all she is willing to make time for. She has filled every area of her life with productivity and leaves no room to feel the warmth or desire to be in a relationship.

This is who Rebecca has become. Every 3-4 months she may entertain some guy that asks for her number while she is getting her morning Frappuccino at Starbucks. But ultimately she never expects relationships to progress because in her mind, all men are the same. Her guard is up so thick and tight that even if a genuinely nice guy approached her, she would likely not notice him. If a genuinely nice guy could take care of her, she would not even recognize it because the persona that she has built does not allow for vulnerability. She goes on about three dates a year, just to have some extra juicy conversation with her girl during their Sunday brunch. If you pay close attention Rebecca and William have switched roles and it couldn't be worse possible timing.

Women mature a lot sooner than men. Therefore, during William's immaturity he usually has connected to a very mature Rebecca. William only realized he is immature by hurting Rebecca. Rebecca has had enough of being hurt and being the good wholesome girl that is constantly disrespected and used. <u>Therefore, when William is maturing Rebecca is retreating.</u> Is this starting to make sense? Rebecca is now starting to turn into everything that she saw in high school and college. Not necessarily the promiscuity and dishonesty, but she saw how constantly being in competition and collecting "things" can ultimately get you affirmation and protection from being hurt. She saw Johnny collect championship football trophies and everyone loved him for it regardless of his personality or character. The same with William, she saw him be respected and revered all over campus because all the girls loved him. Well Rebecca, said now it is my turn to create my identity that will demand that I am respected and never taken advantage of again.

The Alpha Female hears words like submission and immediately are offended. When they hear commentary on scriptures such as 1 Peter 3:7 which says that husbands should give honor to their wives as the weaker vessel, they get offended. Why, because in some way psychologically they feel it suggests that they are not equal and are vulnerable to the leadership of a man. The reality is, that if you peel back the layers of the Alpha Woman's psyche I think you will find that she is only objecting submission because she is viewing it through the lenses of a man who has hurt her in the past. When you really exhaust the definition of the word submission what it really means is "to be taken care of." It does not mean to bow, it does not mean to be a door mat. It means step aside baby and relax, I got this! For all the Alpha Women reading........ that feels much better doesn't it? Didn't that statement connect with you in a very deep way? The word submission does not mean that a man will be lord over you, it means that he will protect you. However, the break down happens when there is no trust. Because where there is no trust, submission becomes bondage. When there is no trust, being delicate becomes weakness. So this is the mindset of a woman who has been hurt by a William. She may entertain a relationship, but it will be on her terms and there will be no room for error at all. We all know this is not realistic and not a healthy crucible for a relationship to grow.

So now the dilemma we have is a willing William and a wounded Rebecca. How do you bring these two back together? Once a woman is hurt so deeply, it is very difficult to regain her trust and cause her to take her guard down. Keep in mind that when I ask the question how do we bring those two back together I am not talking about these two characters literally? I am speaking of who and what these characters represent. William may meet a young lady named Charlotte at the grocery store or at a friend's Labor Day cookout. She is perfect for him. She is beautiful, loyal, and extremely smart. But chances are she has had the same experiences that Rebecca has had in some shape or form and she is looking at William through the same lenses as if she were literally Rebecca. Although he is perfect for her in theory she is extremely guarded and sensitive to the slightest of potential behavior flaws. Remember, the Alpha Female has built a wonderful life (so she thinks) without a man in the picture at all. She is not willing to rock the balance and harmony of her peace for the sake of giving some guy a chance that will likely just hurt her in the long run anyway. The same is true from the male perspective. The Alpha Female can meet a man while she is getting her morning coffee at Starbucks. He is perfect for her. Well dressed, smart, sharp, great sense of humor. However, chances are he has been through the same experiences as William and he is expecting her to be closed off, career focused, and judgmental of his past. This is part of the reason I wrote this book. I want to expose the psychology from both parties perspective so that hopefully we can land somewhere in the middle. If we are not careful, most of us can remain in this cycle for decades. What you must note, once William has "come to himself" and wants genuine relationship there is a very small window of time before he becomes cold and emotionless again. William does not like the feeling of being so vulnerable, especially to one woman. It goes against his core belief system but because of his poor choices in college he had no choice but to face it. Typically, this will send guys like William out into the world with a made up mind to get it right this time. What do they usually find? The "keepers" like Rebecca are now much more appealing to him because he is much more mature. He can now recognize the value of her upbringing and things like her work ethic and overall perspective on the world. However, now the keepers seem to be cold and closed off. They have become Alpha Females and they are extremely sensitive and the slightest little thing can turn them off and make them totally reject him. What this leads to is an eventual total rebellion. Now William is also in the mindset, of what's the use of trying to do the right thing? What's the use in trying to find one women that can meet all my needs? I will never allow one women to have that much power over me again? And he returns to his old ways.

CHAPTER 6

THE MATURITY OF MONOGAMY

William has moved back home and is doing pretty well for himself also. He is now helping his father at the church as an administrator. The church has grown significantly over the years and William is able to put his Business Administration degree to good use. He is now 29 years old and has become more active in his local church. He is really learning a lot and growing by leaps and bounds spiritually. However, of course he has not totally shed all of his promiscuous ways. He still has the occasional slip up but these days it's because of a totally different reason. It is not because he wants to. He actually does not want to and feels horrible every time he falls into pre-marital sex. However, it is a deep routed habit and often times based on the way he carries himself around women it is also convenient. After a certain age and certain experiences casual sex becomes very common and acceptable. Even amongst people of faith. When you eclipse the age of 25 a lot of young adults have been disappointed enough that they don't want the maintenance of a relationship. Learning to trust again, learning to affirm again, learning to be loyal again to something other than their personal goals is not very attractive to this age group. While you can turn off the desire to be in a relationship relatively easy, it is much more difficult to turn off the desire to be sexually active. <u>So in a church full of young adults, yes hookups do happen from time to time. They actually happen much more frequently than marriages do.</u> William is still trying to navigate through all he has learned over the years and now with his growing relationship with God he also has to manage a personal conviction to live a righteous life. However, we must also note that once William became engrafted into the church. He is now in another award system of affirmation. Being with one person is now good, marriage is encouraged, and a calmer cleaner lifestyle is promoted. Even his mother has begun hinting to him that she wants some grandbabies while she still has the energy to play with them. All of these things have gotten William thinking about his past, his present and his future.

Inwardly, he was reminded of the last time he was at such a crossroads. It was the first day of school in the 9th grade and he had choked in front of the prettiest girl in school. His mom helped him sort through that dilemma, now maybe his father can help him through this one. He walks in his dad's office at the church and asked if he wanted to go grab lunch at the local diner. His dad looks at him and jokingly replies are you paying? William says sure and they agree to meet in about an hour. Once at the diner they both place their orders and get through the pleasantries. William's dad a very wise man, tilts his glasses on his nose and says to his son; now what is this all about? You have been working at the church for 5 years now and you have never offered to take me to lunch. "What's on your mind," William's father says? William chuckles and looks at his dad and says "how did you know?" His father responds, "I am your father and an associate pastor I know when someone needs answers." So William takes a deep breath and tries to figure out how to ask his father questions that are probably 15 years overdue. He says to his dad, "I want to talk to you about sex and relationships." His father laughs and says, "that's a great thing to want to know about. I hope I can help you." William, figures out the most non-intrusive question he can think of to ask his father that may shed some light on his dilemma. Dad, "why did you decide to marry mom?" His father sits up a little more erect in his chair, and an undeniable twinkle lurks in his eye and his lips begin to form a half smile. His father says, "this is going to take a little longer than our lunch break but it's going to be worth it." William's father picks up his phone and proceeds to cancel all of his afternoon appointments. The senior ask the junior William to go grab his bible. William runs to the car and gets his bible and returns to the table. His father says, "I am going to tell you why I married your mother but I am also going to give you a lesson on marriage and monogamy." This one lesson is one that many young men never get and many young women wish they did. If you can get a healthy understanding of monogamy and relationships your life will be much richer and more fulfilling. Most young men your age reject the notion of marriage because they feel like they are going to miss out on something. Guys your age only think about sex and having the freedom to go and come as they please. I will teach you today through scripture that a life with your God given mate will unlock blessings that you could never achieve on your own. Marriage is designed to unlock God's favor, not lock you out of earthly pleasures. "Turn to Proverbs 18:22," his father says. "Now read it to me." William reads the words.

22. "He who finds a wife finds a good thing, and obtains favor from the Lord."

This scripture makes me think about why I married your mother, and how the marriage has blessed me. Simply put, when God gave me your mother I obtained favor and blessings that I could have never imagined. When I first got married, I was thinking very similar to how you are thinking right now. Although, I married your mom willingly I can honestly say in the beginning that I wasn't ready at all. I had a very selfish mindset. I felt like I was obligated to marry her because of the pressure I was getting from her family members. Once we got married you were born a couple years later and my life became even more closed in. Instead of maximizing my marriage and enjoying all the pride of having a young beautiful family to lead and strengthen. I spent the first five years of marriage fighting to preserve my liberty and what I understood to be my manhood. I didn't understand at the time that having a family and being honorable did not necessarily equate to the "end of me" but it was actually the completion of me. Fortunately, your mother was very patient with me. Because she was patient with me I learned how valuable she was to my life. When I look back over my life I remember the moment I knew God had specifically made your mother just for me.

When your mother and I got married we didn't have much. We were living in a one bedroom apartment. You were about 3 years old, and your sister was about to be born. I had an hourly job at the local factory and made about two hundred dollars a week. Our family was growing, but our income wasn't. I remember coming home one evening after work and I just sat in the car for about 3 hours. I was so depressed and felt trapped. I didn't have enough money to take care of my family and I also wasn't completely convinced I had done the right thing by getting married so young. That night while sitting in my car I went through so many emotions. I had just finished a long day's work on what seemed to be a fruitless underpaying job. I was hesitant about walking into my reality. Every time I walked into my tiny apartment I felt like a failure and today the anxiety was just too great. I expected your mom to come out to the car and ask me what was wrong. She never did. Eventually, I had enough of my pity party and decided to go into the house. When I came into the house I was met by a note on the dining room table. The note was from your mom. I still have the note to this day. I keep it in my bible. William, read what your mom wrote over 20 years ago to your father. After I read this note, it forever changed how I looked at your mother and marriage. William unfolds the battered and severely worn letter and began to read.

"Hey,

I noticed you sitting in your car and I can tell you had a rough day. I decided to not interrupt you because I know how you like to gather your thoughts. Your dinner is in the oven and I have put William Jr. to bed. When you come to bed tonight, I won't be there. I have decided to spend the night praying for you. I will be in the bathroom because it's the only free space we have. I have already asked our friends next door if you can shower in their apartment. I have packed a bag for you with everything you need. Enjoy your dinner and get a good night sleep. I love you and I believe in you. I am going to talk to God about you all night. Because I am not moved by what I see today, I know we have great things in store because we have such a great man leading us. That man is YOU!!!"

Love,

Sarah

I wish I could say that just reading the words inspired me to immediately feel better. That actually wasn't it at all. I read the letter and yes it was touching. What happened the next morning is what actually changed my life forever. The first thing I need to share with you is that I had not slept well in months. I would toss and turn all through the night. This particular night I slept like a new born baby. It was so odd. Then I woke up so refreshed and I just felt so good. When I awoke I could still hear my wife talking to the Lord about me. I remember thinking wow, she literally stayed up all night praying for me and our family. There were moments she appeared to be crying, then moments she appeared to be laughing and then there were moments she appeared to be just talking. She came out of the bathroom just in time to wake the kids up and get started on breakfast. Before she got started she came in the bedroom and laid beside me and put her head on my chest and said, "it's going to be ok babe." I literally felt like a king in a palace and it dawned on me. I am in a one bedroom apartment in one of the worst parts of town and this women just made me feel like a king in a mansion. As I am literally getting overwhelmed by this amazing sense of peace; the phone rings. I answer the phone and there is this distinguished gentleman is on the other end of the line. He says, "Is this William Jones Sr.?" He then says "My name is Reginald Johnson from corporate. Your name came across my desk, and you were recommended to me as a reliable and hard-working employee. I have been asked to develop a new department and I need a good manager. I think you would be an ideal choice. You will no longer be an hourly employee, but a salaried manager with full benefits. How does that sound?" William Sr. trying to contain himself looks to his wife in amazement and says to the corporate executive "THAT WOULD BE GREAT! It's perfect timing because my wife and I are expecting our second child." Reginald replies, "Welcome to the team you start Monday."

I hung the phone up I could barely hold my composure. I looked to your mother, and said you will not believe what just happened. I shared the great news, and I was thinking that she would have the same excitement. However, she didn't respond nearly the way I thought she would. She just gave me this confident little smirk and went to the kitchen and kept working on breakfast. I followed her in the kitchen and asked her did you hear what I just said? I just got a job I didn't even apply for that comes with benefits and a huge pay increase. We can go to the best hospital in town now to have the baby and we can get a larger home for our growing family. Maybe we can even get a real house with a backyard and everything for the kids. Why aren't you more excited? Your mother looked at me and said something that I never would forget. She said, "William Sr. they are only seeing what I have always seen. I can't celebrate but so much because I am not surprised. I knew you would lead this family into great things. It was just a matter of time that the world sees what I see in you." Not only did your mother expose me to my full potential in business but she also exposed me to the potential of faith. Even though we both grew up in church, I had strayed from the faith. I was in a place in my life that I still believed in God but was honestly not very focused on serving him in any real tangible way. However, your mother so gracefully showed me who God was by the way she treated me. The night when she prayed for me I could tangibly see the difference. I was totally convicted and reminded of God's place in my life. She could have been the typical nagging wife. The night that I was in my car for 3 hours, she could have fussed and created an argument for a hundred different reasons. Why are you in your car so long? Are you on the phone with another woman? Are you doing something wrong? Why can't you come in the house with your family and deal with your problems? Are we not good enough to talk to when you are stressed? She did none of those things. What did your mom do? Cooked dinner, wrote me a thoughtful encouraging note, and decided to have an all-night prayer session for her husband. I knew then that I had married the right woman and that there is strength in marriage. I would never question it again. I began going back to church and my career and our family continued to grow. I am 100% confident I would not be the man I am today without your mom in my life. She brought the best out of me. While I may have impregnated her with you and your sister. Your mother impregnated me with greatness!!!

CHAPTER 7

THE MULTIPLICATION OF MONOGAMY

The junior William is now sitting up in his chair and beginning to lean toward his father. "Wow, that's a great story dad. I didn't realize a woman could make such a difference in your life. The senior William quickly interjects. Not just a woman, but the right woman! God has a woman for you that will make your life better! God's woman for you is worth the wait, and she is worth the sacrifice. William says, "So you are telling me that having one woman; having the right woman is better than having several women and having your freedom? Listen son, marriage is not bondage.....marriage is freedom. Submitting to one woman is a part of God's refining process of a man. The way you relate to your woman is a representation of how you relate to God. This is why God refers to the church as his bride. The order of submission is not an act of weakness. The alternate and accurate definition of submission is an act of strength. The book of Ephesians gives a great lesson on this subject. The senior William tells his son to turn to Ephesians Chapter 5:22-25 for his second lesson about marriage and monogamy. "Read it to me son."

Message Bible

22Wives, understand and support your husbands in ways that show your support for Christ.

23The husband provides leadership to his wife the way Christ does to his church, not by domineering but by cherishing.

24So just as the church submits to Christ as he exercises such leadership, wives should likewise submit to their husbands.

25Husbands, go all out in your love for your wives, exactly as Christ did for the church—a love marked by giving, not getting.

You do not find your full potential through selfishness, you find your full potential in submission. You have not fully lived until you find something or someone worth laying your own personal desires aside. The less individual residue that remains, the more healthy a marriage will be. Many young men see the bondage of marriage, but don't see the greater purpose that is tied to it. Through your sacrifice you find strength, you find discipline, you find that it is better to give than to receive. Your life becomes selfless, and you understand that your decisions are connected to a perpetual deposit for generations to come. In short, your life goes from being all about what you want to what your bride needs. In the midst of this paradox, you find a connection to a deeper, much more meaningful existence. <u>The best version of yourself is always going to be connected to two things. Who you choose to submit to and why?</u> Most of us may not realize it but we all are submitted in some way shape or form. Even the free spirited promiscuous souls that roam freely from one relationship to another are submitted. They are submitted to themselves. They have accepted an idea and approach to life that only seeks immediate personal gratification and the results it produces. Even the friend who is committed to accepting bad advice from unproven, unreliable associates for the sake of friendship, companionship and loyalty is submitted. The young woman who parties every weekend, drinks alcohol heavily, and "turns up" frequently, is submitted to an ideal of a particular lifestyle and the rewards it offers. We all are submitted to certain ideals. There is no escaping it. There is also no escaping the universal truth that whatever philosophy you submit to will determine the outcomes of your life. <u>Submitting to God and submitting to family is the most underrated source of power, focus and</u>

<u>pleasure there is. You just have to learn how it works and tap into it.</u>

God's design of how men and women are to relate to each other is made clear in the beginning of time. "William this is your final lesson for the day." The father asked his son to turn to the book of Genesis 1:28. "Read it for me."

28 And God blessed them, and God said unto them, be fruitful, and multiply, and replenish the earth, and subdue it: and have dominion over the fish of the sea, and over the fowl of the air, and over every living thing that moved upon the earth.

"Son, this is probably the most important lesson you will ever learn about dealing with the opposite sex. Let me ask you a question. Do you love having sex?" William Jr. blushed and refused to answer. His father asked again and emphasized his desire for his son to just be honest. Finally the younger William broke down and said, "Yes dad I love sex." The father said, "You probably have had lots of sex with plenty of different women. I may be busy, but I am not blind. I have been watching you over the years. What would you say if I told you sex was actually a spiritual act?" Now William Jr. is really confused. "How is sex a spiritual act, William Jr. ask. I never feel more disconnected from God than when I am having meaningless casual sex." "Well it's true so pay close attention," William Sr. says.

The first instruction God gave Adam and Eve once they came together was to be FRUITFUL AND MULTIPLY. He ask his son, "How do men and women multiply?" William Jr. says "through sex?" The father says "not exactly, but close." The original multiplication came through words. God spoke things into existence. The earth was God's womb and when He spoke the earth submitted to His "word seed." That's right the original seed was through words. The church has submitted to the word of Jesus which allows us as a global church to multiply. When a women submits to a man sexually, she submits to his words first. That act of sex is the completion of submission through the word released as a seed into the woman's womb. You see there is a male womb and a female womb. This is why I realized who your mother really was in my life, that morning over 20 years ago when I was at my lowest point she spoke a word in my life that began the multiplication in me. I haven't stopped multiplying since. Eve came out of Adam and God had to put him to sleep to create her. This basically means that most men are asleep most of their lives, making bad decisions, using women for sex, cheating, lying, etc. God cannot reveal your Eve to you prematurely. He has to allow you to be asleep, until you are ready to embrace her for who she really is. The other interesting thing to note is that even after Adam was asleep while Eve was being created, he knew exactly who she was when he woke up without any formal introduction. God didn't have to whisper in his ear or show him who she was in a dream. When Adam woke up he knew who his wife was. The same is true for a lot of young men. In most cases, their wives have been close to them for a while. However, he cannot recognize her until he wakes up from his sleep.

Son, you have been asleep and as you are waking up you too will know when your womb has been touched by the right woman's words. Your desire to have sex with all these women, was just a misguided uncontrolled desire to multiply. Sex alone will never fully satisfy you. No matter how much of it you have. You will only be satisfied when you find the woman God intended for you to multiply with. Let's discuss this in a little more depth.

The elder William asks his son have you ever noticed in the book of Genesis how man and woman were created? Most read the story of God forming man from the dust of the ground and breathing into his nostrils and him becoming a living soul. Then we all know what happens next. God says that it's not good that man should be alone and he puts Adam to sleep and creates a woman. Well what about Genesis 1:27?

27 So God created man in His own image; in the image of God He created him; **<u>male and female He created them.</u>**

When I read this scripture, at first it made me scratch my

head a little. God didn't form man of the dust of the ground until Genesis 2:7. God didn't form woman until Genesis 2:22. So how is it that God created man and woman in Genesis 1:27? The answer is in Genesis 2:22 and Proverbs 8:22. Genesis 1:27 suggest the fact that God made man in His image (spirit) and then He formed a man in the flesh. However, the spirit version of man and woman were made at the same time. The natural man that was formed of the dust was a reflection of the spirit man that was created first. When the spirit man was created, the woman assigned to him was already with him. How do we know, because when Adam was formed of the dust his wife was already inside of him? This is confirmed in Genesis 2:22, the bible says Adam was put into a deep sleep and then his wife was pulled out of him. So now, we fast forward to Proverbs 18:22 where it states when a man finds a wife he finds a good thing and obtains favor from the Lord. What more favor can any man have than Adam? Adam was favored in a powerful way because from the very beginning he had his help meet with him. Now, because of him and Eve's fall there was a consequence that is not often talked about. After the fall, man's wife has been separated from him in the natural and he can't recognize her immediately like Adam did. HE HAS TO FIND HER! This was also a part of the fall. When God told Adam his punishment, he pronounced that he would have to work from the sweat of his brow. Now the scripture wasn't just talking about manual labor. I believe the scripture was saying that from now on man will have to work to find their wife, when it was never originally intended that way. Originally the woman that was made for you, the woman that was inside you, the woman that will cause your life to multiply would not have to be found. She would have been known.

Now that you are maturing you are learning what real multiplication is meant to be. It's not about sowing your royal oats as King Jaffi Jafer stated in Coming to America. God is the one who gave you all the desires that you have, but you just have to master them and understand how to channel them properly.

When it comes to women they have a desire for their mind to be stimulated (hear the right things) so that their emotions can be stimulated (feel the right things) so then they can ultimately (surrender to what was heard and felt) physical stimulation (sex). In that order is really God's natural design or intention for you to multiply. The problem is because no one teaches this; many women's requirements for their emotions to be stimulated are not very profound. They don't understand that sex is totally related to submission. When a woman sleeps with a man, she is ultimately saying I submit to this man's ability to multiply my being. I am submitting to his ability to maximize the fruit I am able to bear in this lifetime.

However, most will settle for submitting to the feeling of sex opposed to the purpose of sex. This way of thinking, keeps the dysfunctional cycle going. Women will exchange their body for a weak word, and men will offer their seed for a weak womb.

William asks his son to give him a napkin. He begins to write on the napkin. He says "This is what God showed me about ten years ago." This is how multiplication works. God spoke his word and the earth submitted. Jesus spoke his word and the church submitted. Man speaks his word and the woman submitted. All three yield multiplication that is generational and profitable for all mankind.

God/Word – Womb/Earth - MULTIPLY

Jesus/Word – Womb/Church - MULTIPLY

Man/Word – Womb/Woman – MULTIPLY

What's interesting to note, is that the easier it is to access a woman's womb typically means someone else has already accessed it and abused it. Sometimes before the multiplication can begin, healing has to take place. Likewise, the easier it is for a man to release his seed typically indicates that he has some healing to do also. This usually means that he hasn't learned the value of his harvest as of yet so he is willing to trade his God given birthright for immediate gratification and feelings instead of fruit. There is a bible story about that as well, but we will save it for another day. When a man doesn't know himself, he will let society define him through vain affirmation and ideals to promote his ego. The young William is listening to his father's wisdom and is absorbing it all. He looks at his dad and says, "This all makes so much sense. I just wish I had not wasted so much time, and I've hurt so many women and I've made so many mistakes." His father just laughed and said, "Son we all have a different journey of how we mature." Although I know you have many regrets, you cannot change the past. Instead of focusing on your errors, focus on what you learned in the process. Maybe one day, you can sit down with a young man who is having some of your same struggles and help him understand himself a little better. There may even be a young lady in distress and struggling with her identity. Maybe you can help her when she has tears in her eyes because the love of her life isn't focused and has anxiety about settling down. As of result of everything you have loved, lost and learned on that day you can look at her right in her eyes and from a place of wholeness and overcoming say "This is WHY HE WON'T MARRY YOU!!!!!"

ABOUT THE AUTHOR

Alexander J. Patrick is the pastor of Liberation Church International. He is a proud husband, father and spiritual leader to many. Pastor Jay as known by many has a deep desire and gifting to share the gospel message in unique and relevant ways. Many say his wisdom is unparalleled for someone his age. This book is one of many that will serve as a resource to reform communities and families back to wholeness and health. Thank you for supporting this project and once you are done, please spread the word about this life changing project. It is our belief that this is a message that the world needs to hear.